STEP-by-STEP

SCIENCE

Flowering Plants

Chris Oxlade

Illustrated by Stuart Lafford
and Shirley Tourret

W
FRANKLIN WATTS
LONDON • SYDNEY

© Franklin Watts 1998

First Published in Great Britain by Franklin Watts
96 Leonard Street London EC2A 4XD
This edition 2002

Franklin Watts Australia
56 O'Riordan Street
Alexandria, Sydney
NSW 2015

ISBN 0 7496 4519 9 (pbk)

10 9 8 7 6 5 4 3 2

Dewey Decimal Classification 581.1

A CIP catalogue record for this book is available from the British Library

Printed in Dubai

Planning and production by Discovery Books Ltd
Design: Ian Winton
Edited by Helena Attlee
Consultant: Jeremy Bloomfield

Photographs: Bruce Coleman: page 4 bottom (Dr F Sauer), 6 (John Shaw),
10 (Jules Cowan), 12 bottom (John Shaw), 20 top (Jules Cowan), 26 (Jane Burton),
27 top (P Clement), bottom (John Shaw); Robert Harding: page 8 (Adam Woolfitt),
19 (Robert Lundy), 20 bottom, 28 (Gavin Hellier), 31 (Mark Mawson); NHPA: page 13 bottom
(Jany Sauvanet), 24 (David Woodfall), 25 (Stephen Krasemann); Oxford Scientific Films: page 11 top
(Scott Camazine), 12 top (G I Bernard), 13 top (Robert Tyrell), 22 (Tim Shepherd), 23 bottom (Tim
Shepherd); Alex Ramsay: page 4 top, 29; Tony Stone: page 11 bottom (Ron Boardman), 14 (Mike
McQueen), 21 (W and D Macintyre), 23 top (Michael Busselle); ZEFA: cover.

Contents

Plants and Flowers

Most kinds of plants have flowers. You have probably seen roses flowering in the summer and enjoyed their beautiful scent.

But did you know that trees are flowering plants, too?

In fact, any plant that has a flower is called a flowering plant. Flowering plants grow all over the world. They can be found everywhere, from cold, windy mountain tops to hot, dry deserts.

Flowering plants grow best of all in tropical places, where it is hot and wet all year round. Look at all of the different flowers in this picture.

Parts of a Plant

There are hundreds of flowers in this meadow. Although they are very different colours, shapes and sizes, they all have the same parts.

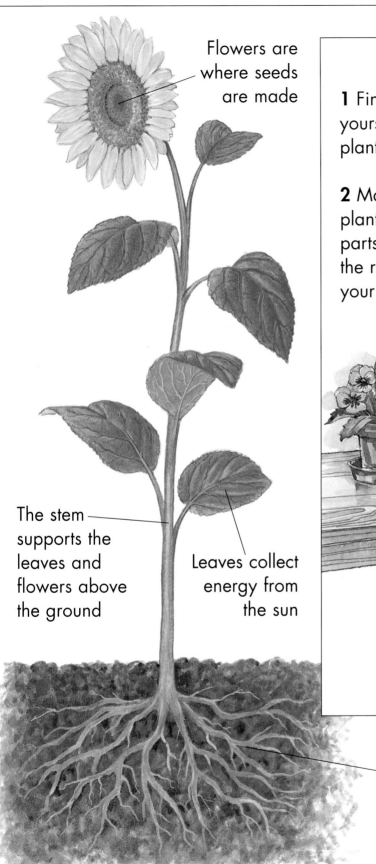

Flowers are where seeds are made

The stem supports the leaves and flowers above the ground

Leaves collect energy from the sun

Roots grow under the ground. They support the plant and collect the water and **minerals** from the soil.

DRAW A PLANT

1 Find a flowering plant for yourself. You can either use a pot plant or a plant from outside.

2 Make a careful drawing of your plant, labelling all of the different parts. (You may not be able to draw the roots as this would mean pulling your plant up!)

Flowers

A plant's flowers are where its seeds are made. Later, these seeds will grow into new plants.

Most plants flower during the spring and summer. In this picture, some of the flowers are in bud, some are flowering and others have already flowered.

A few plants, like these snowdrops, flower during the winter.

The first things that we notice when we look at a flower are its **petals**. Oil in the petals gives the flower its sweet scent.

The **sepals** protect the flower bud before it opens.

The flower has male parts – called **stamens** – and a female part called the **carpel**. Both parts are needed to make seeds.

Sepals

Carpel

Stamens

Petals

Nectary

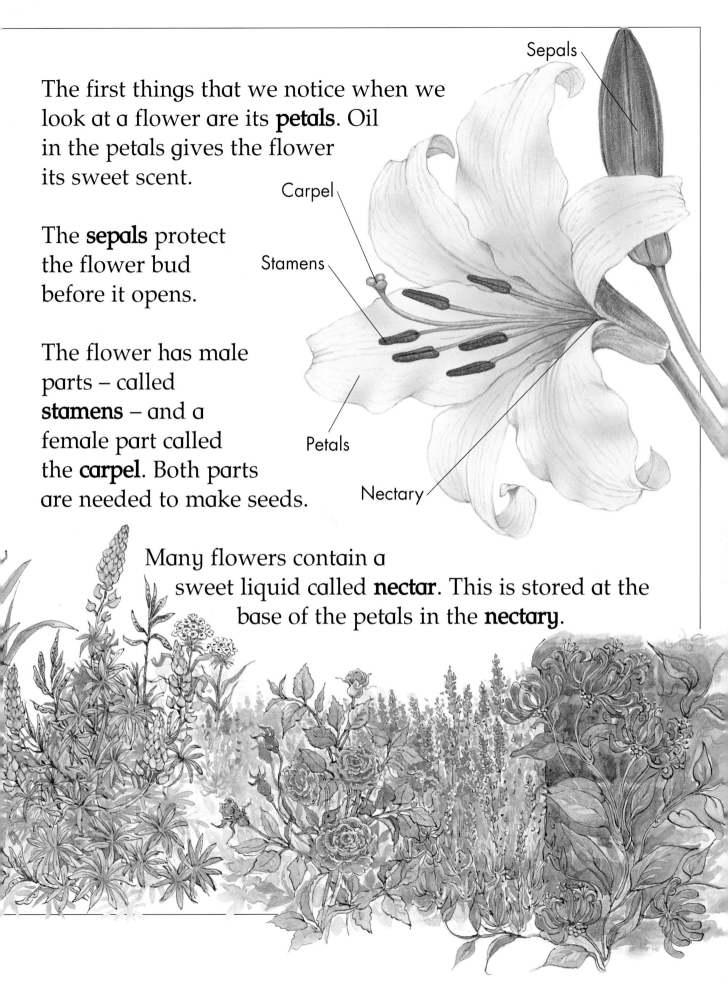

Many flowers contain a sweet liquid called **nectar**. This is stored at the base of the petals in the **nectary**.

Pollination

This tulip has very dark brown stamens. Can you see the carpel at the centre of the flower?

The stamens make a powdery dust called **pollen**. To make a seed, pollen from the stamens of one flower must reach the carpel of another. This is called **pollination**.

Most plants are pollinated by pollen from another plant of the same kind. This is called cross-pollination. A few plants can pollinate themselves. This is called self-pollination.

The picture on the right shows the pollen from the stamens already on the carpel.

Pollen grains come in many different shapes but they are always too small to see properly without a magnifying glass.

This is what the pollen grains look like through the lens of a microscope.

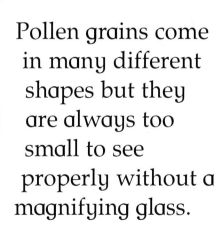

Pollen Carriers

How does pollen from one flower reach the female parts of another? Flowering plants need help to spread their pollen. Some plants use the wind to carry the pollen from one flower to another. Can you see the cloud of pollen around this grass?

Many flowers are pollinated by insects, birds or other animals.

This bee has been feeding on the nectar inside a flower. It is covered in pollen from the flower's stamens. Some of this pollen will rub off on the carpel of the next flower that it visits. Other insects pollinate flowers in the same way.

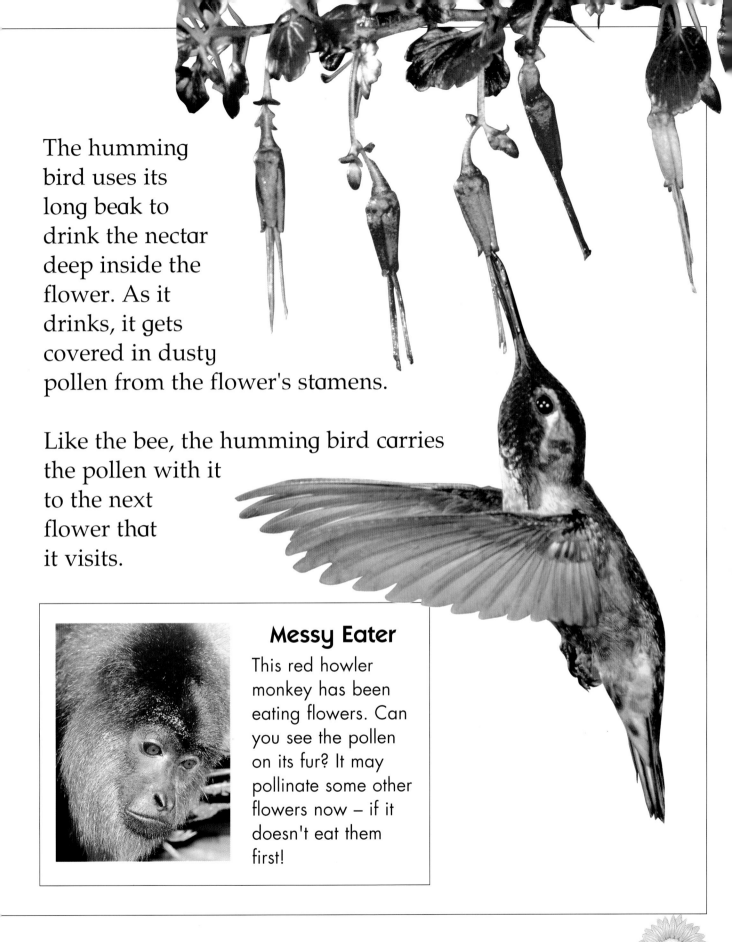

The humming bird uses its long beak to drink the nectar deep inside the flower. As it drinks, it gets covered in dusty pollen from the flower's stamens.

Like the bee, the humming bird carries the pollen with it to the next flower that it visits.

Messy Eater

This red howler monkey has been eating flowers. Can you see the pollen on its fur? It may pollinate some other flowers now – if it doesn't eat them first!

Seeds

Once a flower has been pollinated a seed begins to grow inside it. Now the flower has done its job and the petals start to die away.

All seeds, even the very tiny ones, contain the parts which will grow into a new plant and the food that the plant will need when it is very young.

Some seeds grow inside hard cases. Each of these coconuts could grow into a new palm tree.

Others grow inside a soft, fleshy case called a fruit. This tree is covered with plums. Inside each plum is one large seed.

Some kinds of seed, such as peas, grow in pods. Even though we think of peas as vegetables, they are really a fruit.

Some plants produce seeds only once and then die. We call these annual plants. Plants that produce seeds year after year are called perennials.

Scattering Seeds

Once seeds have formed, they need to be scattered. In cool climates this usually happens in the autumn. If all of the seeds grew into plants on the same patch it would soon become too crowded.

These sycamore tree seeds have tiny wings which help them to fly along on the wind.

When birds eat these juicy berries, they eat the seeds inside them, too. This does the seeds no harm. They pass through the bird's stomach and fall onto the ground in its droppings, far away from the plant where they were formed.

Inside this prickly burr is the seed of the burdock. It spreads by sticking to the fur of passing animals or to people's clothes.

Squirrels store nuts for the winter by burying them in the ground. Sometimes they forget where their store is and the nuts grow up into new trees.

A Plant is Born

In spring the days grow longer and warmer. Seeds that have been lying in the cold ground all winter begin to grow. This is called germination.

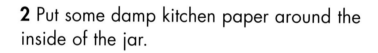

This seed is about to germinate.

The outer case of the seed has broken open.

A root is growing down to anchor the new plant in the soil.

The first leaves are beginning to grow.

GROW YOUR OWN BEANS

1 Put a little water into the bottom of a jam jar.

2 Put some damp kitchen paper around the inside of the jar.

3 Now put a broad bean seed between the glass and the paper.

4 Look at your seed every day. Draw it or write down what is happening to it.

5 When the roots and the stem of your bean have developed, it can be planted outside in the ground or in a pot.

Some kinds of seeds lie in the ground for many years before they germinate. The seeds of the lotus flowers in this pool can wait for 2,000 years before germinating.

Sowing Seed

This farmer is planting seeds. The seeds go in neat rows in the ground. This makes the plants easy to harvest when they have grown.

Leaves

All flowering plants must have leaves. Each different kind of plant has different leaves.

This plant lives in the desert where it hardly ever rains. Its pointed leaves have a waxy surface which stops them drying out.

This alpine plant grows high up in the mountains. It has tiny leaves that will not be damaged by the wind. The hairs on its leaves protect them from the sun's heat.

The leaves of the water lily are shaped like rafts. They float easily on the surface of the water.

Although there are so many different kinds of leaf, the leaves of all flowering plants have the same parts.

Below is a picture of a walnut leaf.

The leaf is flat and thin so that as much sunlight as possible hits its surface.

These tiny holes are called **stomata**. They allow gases to pass in and out of the leaf.

Tiny tubes called **veins** carry water and food around the leaf.

Making Food

Sun

Flowering plants are like us – they need food to live and grow. We have to eat food but plants can make their own.

Plants use sunlight to turn a gas called **carbon dioxide** from the air, and water from the ground into a sugary food. This process is called **photosynthesis**.

Leaves absorb carbon dioxide

Water and minerals taken up by roots

Inside a plant's leaves there is a substance called chlorophyll. It colours leaves green in summer. Chlorophyll **absorbs** the sunlight that is needed for photosynthesis.

In autumn a tree's leaves begin to dry up and die. They change colour as the chlorophyll inside them breaks down.

Chlorophyll is stored in the tree throughout the winter, while the tree's branches are bare.

Sending Down Roots

At the bottom of a plant's stem, hidden under the ground, are its roots. Roots collect water and minerals from the soil. They also anchor the plant in the ground.

Main root growing down into ground

Near the tip of each root are tiny root hairs which collect water and minerals from the soil

The root cap protects the end of the root as it pushes through the soil

Mangroves grow in the salty swamps close to tropical seas. Some of the trees' roots anchor them to the wet ground. Others grow upwards so that they stick out above the water.

Unusual Roots

Orchids live high up on the branches of other trees. Their roots cannot reach the ground. Instead they dangle down absorbing all of the water that they need from the moist air of the rainforest.

ROOTING A CUTTING

Some plants can be grown from cuttings. You can try this for yourself using a geranium.

1 Cut a short length of stem from your geranium. Choose a side shoot with a couple of leaves at the end of it.

2 Half fill a clean jar with warm water. Put the cutting into the jar so that the bottom end sits in the water.

3 After a few days tiny new roots will have grown from the stem.

4 When the cutting has strong roots you can plant it in a pot of its own. You have made a new plant!

Meat-Eaters

Some flowering plants cannot make enough food by photosynthesis. They have to get extra **nourishment** by eating insects. We call these carnivorous plants.

The leaves of the Venus flytrap snap shut around the unfortunate insect inside. The plant dissolves the insect's body with **digestive** juices.

The leaves of the pitcher plant are filled with liquid. Insects, attracted to the plant by its sweet smelling nectar, fall into the liquid at the bottom and drown.

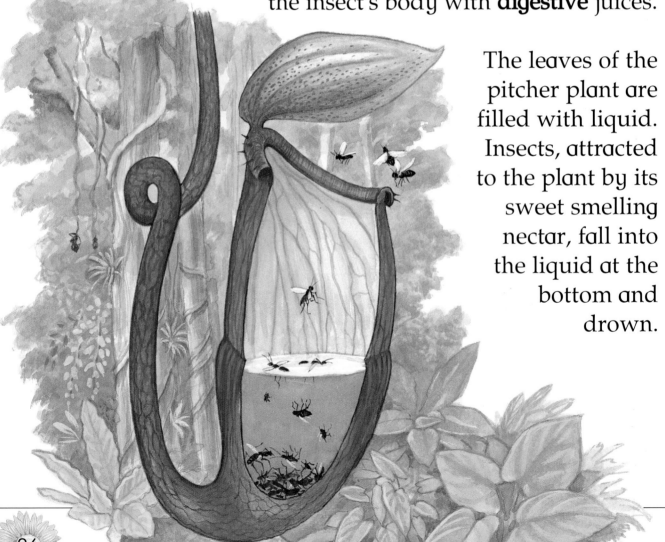

The butterwort on the right and the sun-dew below have sticky leaves. If an insect lands on them it cannot escape and the plant will slowly digest it.

Stems

A plant's stem supports its leaves and flowers above the ground. Sometimes the leaves and flowers grow all the way along the stem, and sometimes they grow only at the end of the stem. The plant's roots grow from the bottom of the stem.

Useful Stems

Bamboo plants have thick stems. When they are cut they harden quickly and can be put to many different uses. These Chinese builders have made a strong scaffolding tower from bamboo.

Some plants have fragile stems and need support like this clematis.

Tiny tubes inside the stem carry water from the roots to the leaves. Other tubes carry food from the leaves to the rest of the plant.

CHANGING COLOUR

This experiment will show you how water from the roots is carried to all the different parts of the plant.

1 Fill a glass with water and add a few drops of red food colouring to it.

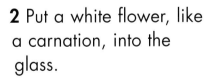

2 Put a white flower, like a carnation, into the glass.

3 Look at the flower after about half an hour. What has happened to it?

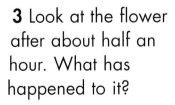

Storing Food

Look at the picture below. These vegetables are all parts of flowering plants. They are all good to eat.

Cabbages and lettuces are leaves. Carrots and parsnips are swollen roots. Rhubarb and leeks are stems.

Some plants have underground stems which swell up when the plant's leaves die in winter. This is where the plant stores food which it needs to grow again in the spring. Potatoes are swollen underground stems, called tubers.

An onion is an underground store of food called a bulb. It is a ball of thick, fleshy leaves with a small stem at the bottom.

Many garden flowers, like these daffodils, also grow from bulbs. You must not eat these bulbs. They are poisonous.

J129, 343

Glossary

Absorb: To take in water or another substance

Carbon dioxide: A gas in the air which plants need to live

Carpel: The female part of a flower

Digestive: To do with digestion, the means by which an animal or plant absorbs the useful substances in food

Minerals: Substances in the soil that plants need to grow

Nectar: A sugary liquid inside a flower that insects drink

Nectary: The place in the centre of a flower where nectar is made

Nourishment: The substances that a plant needs to live

Petals: The parts of a flower which are often brightly coloured to attract insects and birds

Photosynthesis: The process which plants use to make food using light from the sun

Pollen: Tiny particles from the male part of a flower (the stamens) which make the flower pollinate if they reach the female part of the flower (the carpel)

Pollination: When pollen from the stamens of one flower reaches the carpel of another flower

Sepals: Green flaps, like petals, which protect a flower before it opens

Stamens: The male part of a flower, where pollen is made

Stomata: Tiny holes on the underneath of a leaf which let gases get in and out of the leaf

Vein: A narrow tube inside a leaf along which liquid flows

Index